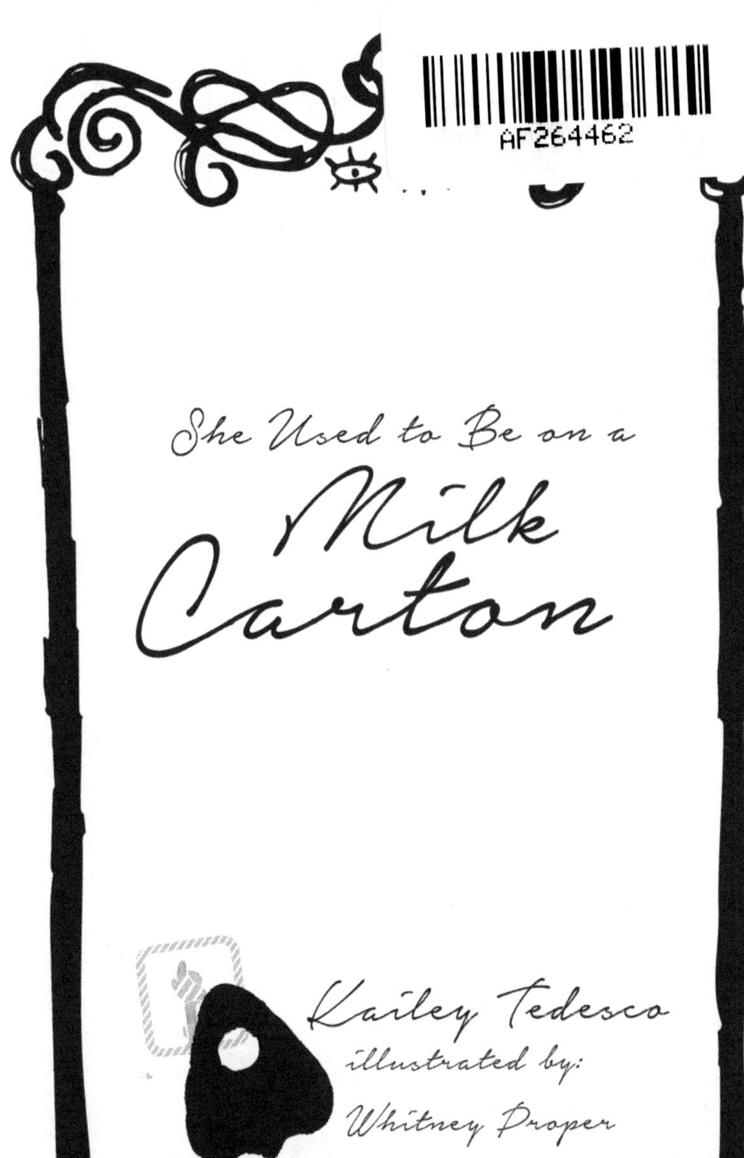

She Used to Be on a Milk Carton

Kailey Tedesco

illustrated by:

Whitney Proper

Publisher's Cataloging-in-Publication Data

Tedesco, Kailey.
    She used to be on a milk carton / written by Kailey Tedesco /
illustrated by Whitney Proper
    ISBN: 978-0-9882061-6-8

1. Poetry: General 2. Poetry: American - General I. Title
II. Author III. Illustrator

Library of Congress Control Number: 2018933121

[Accolades for Kailey Tedesco]

Accolades for Kailey Tedesco

"In the dark glittering magic of these poems, Kailey Tedesco tears the caul away from the female experience, all at once unique and familiar – its potential victim-ness transformed into a thing of power: a girlhood gone macabre among exorcisms and séances; a girlhood more dynamic with each talisman – the planchettes, tarot cards, a "mood ring filled with bees"; a girlhood made beastly in the realm of minotaurs and witchery."
- Genevieve Betts, author of *An Unwalled City*

"The poems in *She Used to Be on a Milk Carton* are like visceral mood pieces, throbbing, breathless and heady. Where past and present intersect, where the body and the mind are both at odds and at once intimate lovers, these poems suspend, magically and surprisingly, what we know of the shadowy and hidden world we inhabit. These poems are scarlet, heavy brocaded curtains, in dark Victorian rooms where spirits both real and imagined might lurk. Wo(man) and nature, things seen, unseen, imagined and conjured, feminine and feminist, these poems will challenge your emotional status quo, but most definitely, in all the ways that will make the heart inside your chest beat like a drum."
- Michelle Reale, Author of *All These Things Were Real: Poems of Delirium Tremens* and *Birds of Sicily*

"Kailey Tedesco's poetry builds haunted Victorian dollhouses in the eternal moment where childish innocence collides with grown-up wickedness. It's like eavesdropping on Little Red Riding Hood & the Big Bad Wolf's cool older sister as they run off toward a night of Dionysian revelry. Like a Catholic school-girl's epiphany, on the day of her first Holy Communion, that she's actually the reincarnation of a murdered bordello madam from New Orleans. *She Used to Be on a Milk Carton* is an ideal collection of all these weird, wild, wonderful things, with an emphasis on Kailey's exquisite command of the realms which border the sensual and the spiritual."
- Joseph P. O'Brien, editor of FLAPPERHOUSE

"Part ghost girl's Bildungsroman and part grimoire, *She Used to Be on a Milk Carton* is a decadent, mesmeric, dangerous collection. Kailey Tedesco's poems will unsettle you. They will lead you off the path through the untouched snow to the wolf's den, rip your curls out, but hand you roses. They will cut like broken glass then shimmer for you in their own moon-light, brimming with mood rings and suicides, rabbit holes and rosaries, bees, bones, blood, and illusions."
- Jessie Janeshek, author of *The Shaky Phase* and *Invisible Mink*

"Kailey Tedesco's *She Used to Be on a Milk Carton* wishes to be found. These poems baptize us in a low-lying swamp, illuminated with torches and smelling of lavender. Dreamy, contentious, and drenched in a gown of dogmatic reversals, Tedesco sacrifices all but the soul, in hopes that one day the exhumation will be as glorious as the birth."
- Josh Dale, writer and publisher at Thirty West Publishing House

edited by:

[edited by:]

Matt Johnstone,
Robyn Leigh Lear,
& Lance Umenhofer

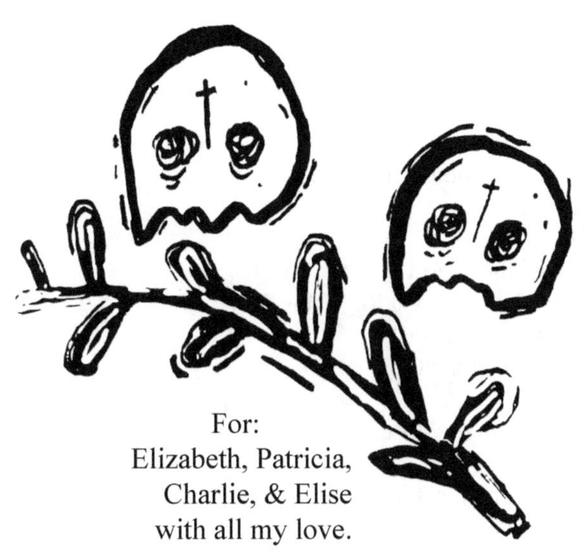

For:
Elizabeth, Patricia,
Charlie, & Elise
with all my love.

Contents

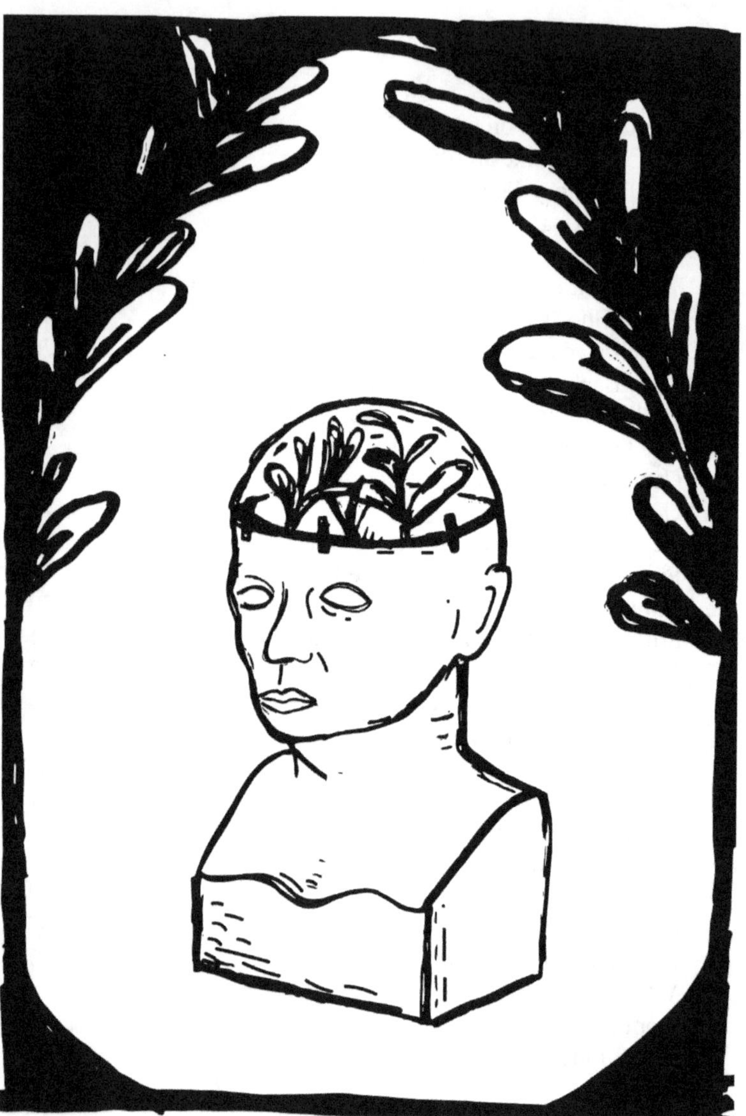

The Place Before Crossing Over

I am in a place with fox hides
firing against the side of
my soaked back –

I think that I am a rose
with holiness, or else
rapture flowering

from me in expulsions. The act
of lounging half
way through this hole

is violent & I am not sure
when I last spoke
with mother on the telephone,

but I'm interested
in hot winds & forest animals
whose mouths drip & scroll

like mirrors. The art
of becoming myself parallels
the first time I touched myself

in that both carry the medium's
apathy towards death as a cover
for her wish that death,

She Used to Be on a Milk Carton

like everything else,
might crack up sometime
& glimmer off like flame-

licked loti riding
the cackle of sea.

Kailey Tedesco

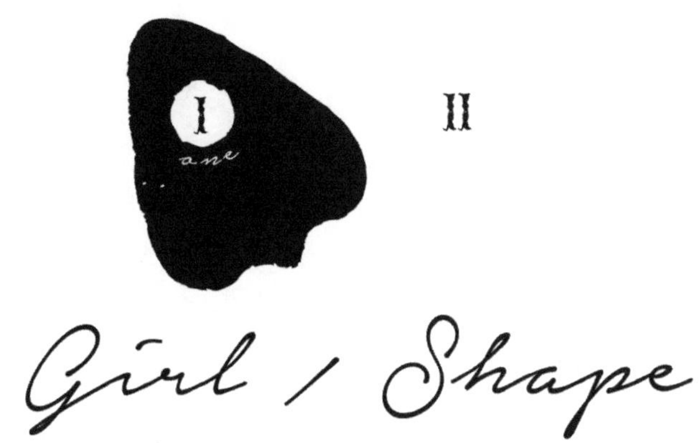

I
one

II

Girl / Shape

[Girl / Shape]

The Vampire Who Said He Was You

Inside – there is a snake & it
shines – I grab & grab
but my hand is sour candy.

You gave the snake
to me – a present.
I said thank you & peeled
the wax off
the black moon (shiny

& makes my nose run dark).
The snake is wrapped around
galaxies inside me, sucking
at pink stars & gutty jupiter.

I was wrapped with caul – a still-
birth still breathing.
You chewed the feathers
off me & bit down.

Now I see shapes coagulate
from my body – a vision. Always
red figures or black in certain
moonlight.

I will never turn thirteen –
I die, I die, I die
& you already
know it.

I had no idea
you smelled blood
on me
even then.

St. Rose of Benevolent Menses

*You might consider the idea of tasting your own menstrual
blood; if it makes you sick, you've got a long way to go, baby.*
– Germaine Greer

I can feel her baubles modest on my
breasts. She came like a toothed fairy
to put euphemisms between my legs.

Shove the moon up your crotch.
Let it light the way.

I am a generator of universes –
I wear it on my lips.

I am a red woman drinking peony
martinis. Let me cast a spell
each month.

Pull hatched grass
from the guff of earth. Turn the world
to stickers, arrange them in a book.

Kailey Tedesco

Purity Ring

I can tell you
lack the rigidity of a locked door –

You are the word for emptying
rings from each finger
into a ceramic bowl like a stream
of urine.

I stay awake praying to Christ
in a bronze doze & lament
the sun-dried palms hoisted
over His shoulders –

I ask Him if you, too, know
the feel of carrying the infant
of your own life – a breastbone
nuzzling to make you lonely

against the babes of resurrection?
Will you smile when they track
your milk's cologne & call it theirs?

Obituary for Another Mermaid Girl

I offer a ghost in glittering
oral & salt to shut
her casket –

I am the evident
cause of death & she is
my elderflower familiar –
one cup

of placenta
will siamese
the lungs & that is
a promise – you have

my word, my hand,
my sympathetic
magic. How many

times do I need to tell you
we're all a child
rolling downhill & rolling,

rolling underneath –
dirt & water choke
similarly so it's easy

to remember
how to swim.

GirlStuff.com

The stuff that can navigate eggs & everything after.

You think you're the creator, but
slippered feet know how to use
the moon as their compass
when the time comes.

The makeup is the apparition of boa
feathers lost in bottom drawers, clear as UFOs
smiling across the meniscus of your eye.

Its X marks the birth spot. You can &
will tear its rag-doll seams, but beware
the onslaught of beads hosing out & over
like a magician pulling scarves from
sleeves.

It's you. It's me. It's the fan that blows
her hair back in your dreams.

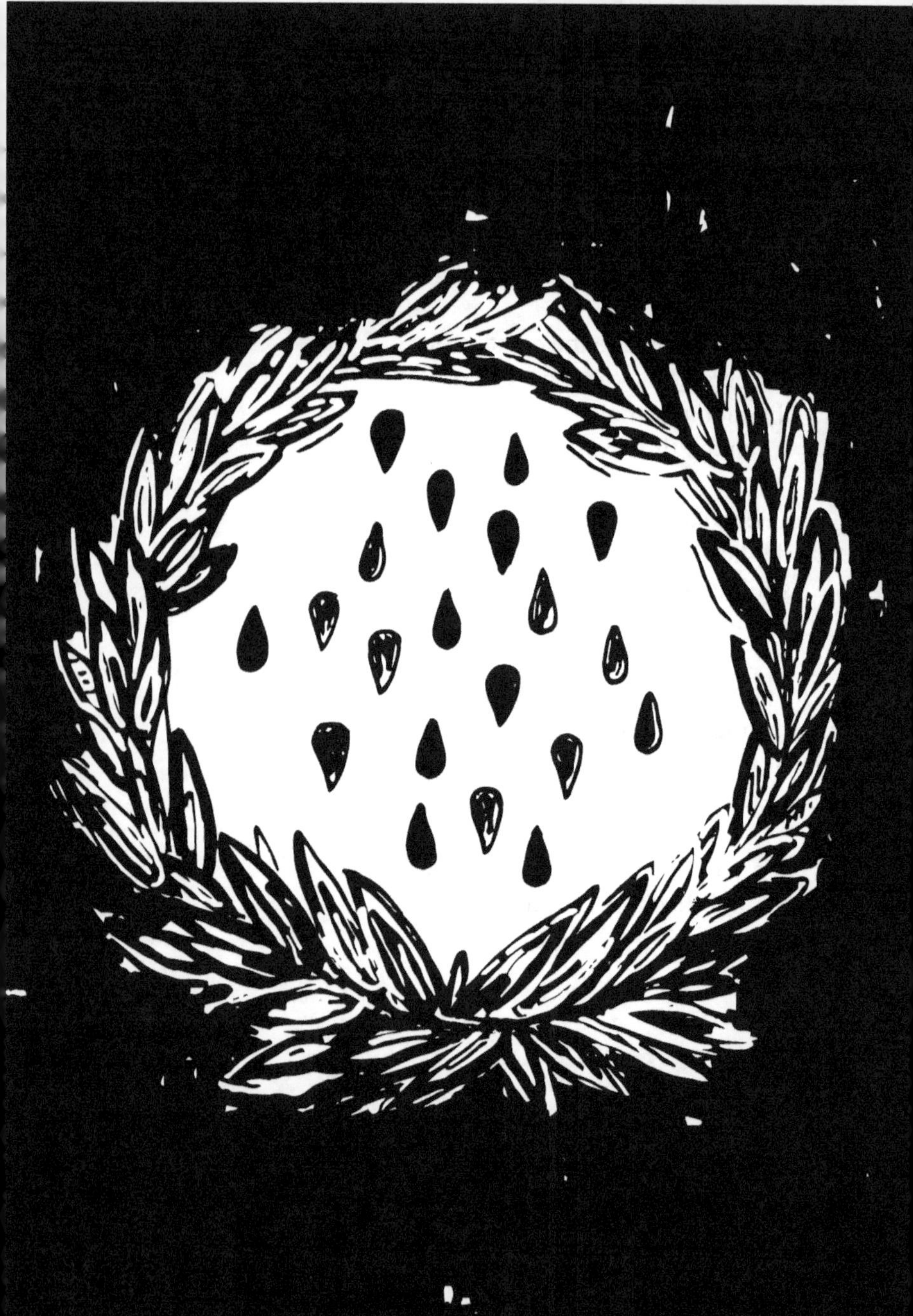

On My Girl

You think death has ripped you forever apart.
– Vada Sultenfuss

Around the time of mother's hemorrhage
my mood ring filled with bees.

They slept when I kissed him – my mouth
honeyed with amber.

Willow leaf-masks & citronella
will remind me of wanting to be close enough

to touch the bumps on his head – soft braille
to signify still-developing phrenology.

It was the one day in hot green light
that I understood flesh reason,

before the bees hatched, before they pounded him
& broke his glasses, before my mother

died, & before the sex that made me
later make the bees.

She Saved the World A Lot
[She Saved the World A Lot]

If I could have one do-over, I'd have vampires
there in vamp-face crouching over

glass & your own slow breaths. You'd be
sired by morning. Fresh-faced as you pluck

asphalt from your elbows, a mug
of blood in your hands.

How strange to think of you outliving me now –
thrust into memory just enough so as not to wake it.

I wonder if you clawed into your own heaven. Did your
knuckles ache against the tingle of crabgrass?

I wonder why I can't
find you now.

My Eye, Haunted by a Rag Time Girl

        In a gas mask – jazz-age roaches swarm
over cold tea at the witching hour & her curdled

gown trails over my cornea,
sobs gulp & spiral –

I don't know which tears are mine. I'm reminded
of the bomb-crumbs. My lids close & I feel

the pulse of old gramophones keeping
me up all night with ectoplasm in my

eyelids. My eyelids are only
a planchette she twitches over time.

If I could bring myself to blink,
she might finally die.

Water, Sweet and Nasty

For Elisa Lam, who found herself stuck in a cistern.

Elisa is inside a glass of tap
water – danced & infused.

Cecil guests swish her around
mouths, dip bristles in her tongue –

high tea & black slick falls
over hair, head, & palms.

Front desk thanks guests
for understanding she's been in
the water tank, days on end –

a puddle of bloat at the bottom
like a wreath of darjeeling.

Asbury Park in the Off-Season

The cheshire-tooth simpers away
& the ferris wheel, empty,
persists against grey winds.

Broken glass skitters across
linoleum like dice on a table –
it peoples the abandoned casino.

The shore in its pure being –
square-scene polaroid
left to develop in the
November morning.

Huddled on a bench – I
exist with the warmth of
cheeseburgers, dazzled

by the bare horizon
bathing in the sun.

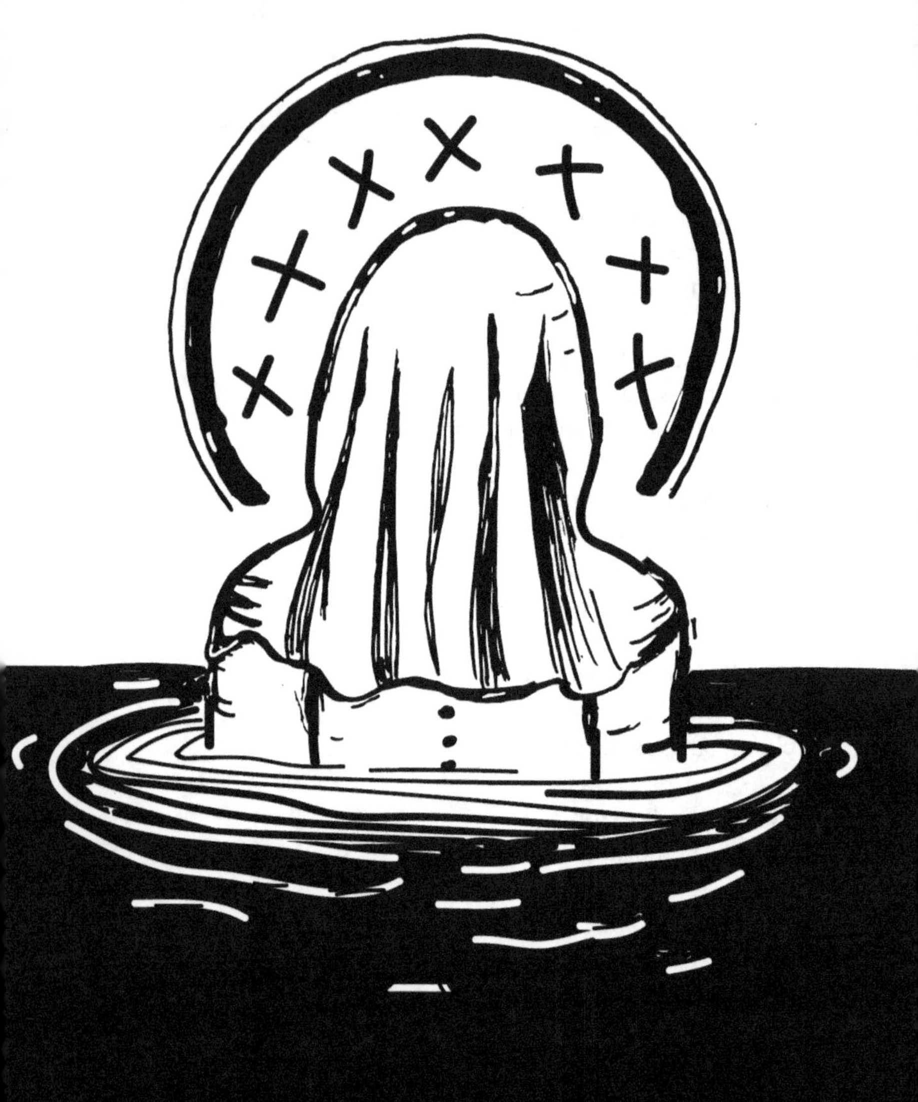

Dark Water

Light decides to float on the surface instead of looking inside. You should have seen the way Grandma ran & dove all in one motion when you went under. One minute you're flashing Little Mermaid floats, the next you're vanished in a way that makes me question object permanence. But you bobbed back up before any of us could even get to you. Hands in the air as if to say I am the drowner, not the drownee here. Still, I wondered how we would have found you in all that copper water, lead-heavy & stamped with everything it wants to devour.

On Flowers in the Attic

Where was that fragile, golden-fair Dresden doll I used to be?
Gone. – V.C. Andrews

The sun is something I rarely visit –
I must keep it tucked beneath
my skin, smuggled opals

to be emptied into the cedar-garden.
Let the sputtering drops enter the boards
soiled with breakfast arsenic.

Dandelions & buttercups will not grow
among these planks, but my chest's
own expansions will soon shrink the room.

I will wear this attic as a blouse, Alice-
style. You will help me to unzip it –
together we'll watch the walls crumble
like laundry.

Shrine
[Shrine]

Eureka's rosary is on the street where Eureka used to be. Not quite dead, but dreaming of astrology on her tongue. In this world of velvet – the Mother with arms & legs spread to grasp once more at the expanding chanterelle of ghosts. Sometimes there are grey children or grey candles agape at the dead-fish poke of her smile. At others, a flagellating playbill & rainworm ballet shoes. In this castle, we refuse to put things where they belong. This is all because a man touched the moon years ago, as that man was wont to do. Yet, we cannot blame a love of full pockets alone. Mood rings will always return fertile with the smeared hologram of Eureka & her bodies. This is a promise.

There Are Creatures in These Woods of Mine
[There Are Creatures in These Woods of Mine]

The wolves & I speak freely to one another – I crouch naked
beneath the gristle of their chins & take one fast bite, metallic
and dry.

I molt my threadbare skin, dancing with the swollen
pines – my feet safe with mud. I do not fear
beasts the way I fear my own open legs in

mirrors or the blue echo of your television peering
through my window. In my woods, I can remove
my dress.

    In your woods, there's only dead dirt & a sun
that stinks of perspiration. In your woods,
my body & the stars stay

fogged & I leave
my wolves at home.

Kailey Tedesco

The Planets Star in a Burlesque

Mars wears fishnets, Venus
pouts a red lip before the
vanity bulbs of night.

Mercury's all flesh in
her pink silk dress, boasting
thigh-high side-slits –

Zip this. Zip this.
Sun's lacquered fingers
slide up the back of

her neck, then linger.
In row 5-D of the moon's
mezzanine, we can see her

sequin-gowned
Allez up! & drapes the
dark in her gold chiffon.

Neptune milks 'em
with tassels swing
swing swinging so close

you see perfume smoke –
a showstopper, spotlight
ballyhoo follows Mars'

boa, calls us rovers, belts out
over sax thunder booming do-
da-do-da – oh!

A drumroll from the clouds
before Venus cries out –
a beat – and Earth quakes.

Depression for Catholics

Think Mother Mary
at the prom.

If you're wearing white,
quickly imagine everything else red.

Try to walk through that red world
without getting wet.

You can't help but to think of *The Exorcist*
as you take communion bread.

Actually, you can't help but to think
of *The Exorcist* most days.

They tell you the dark has a face.
You can't see the face, but it wants you.

You'll lose count after three *Our Fathers*.
It won't matter. You're up for the night.

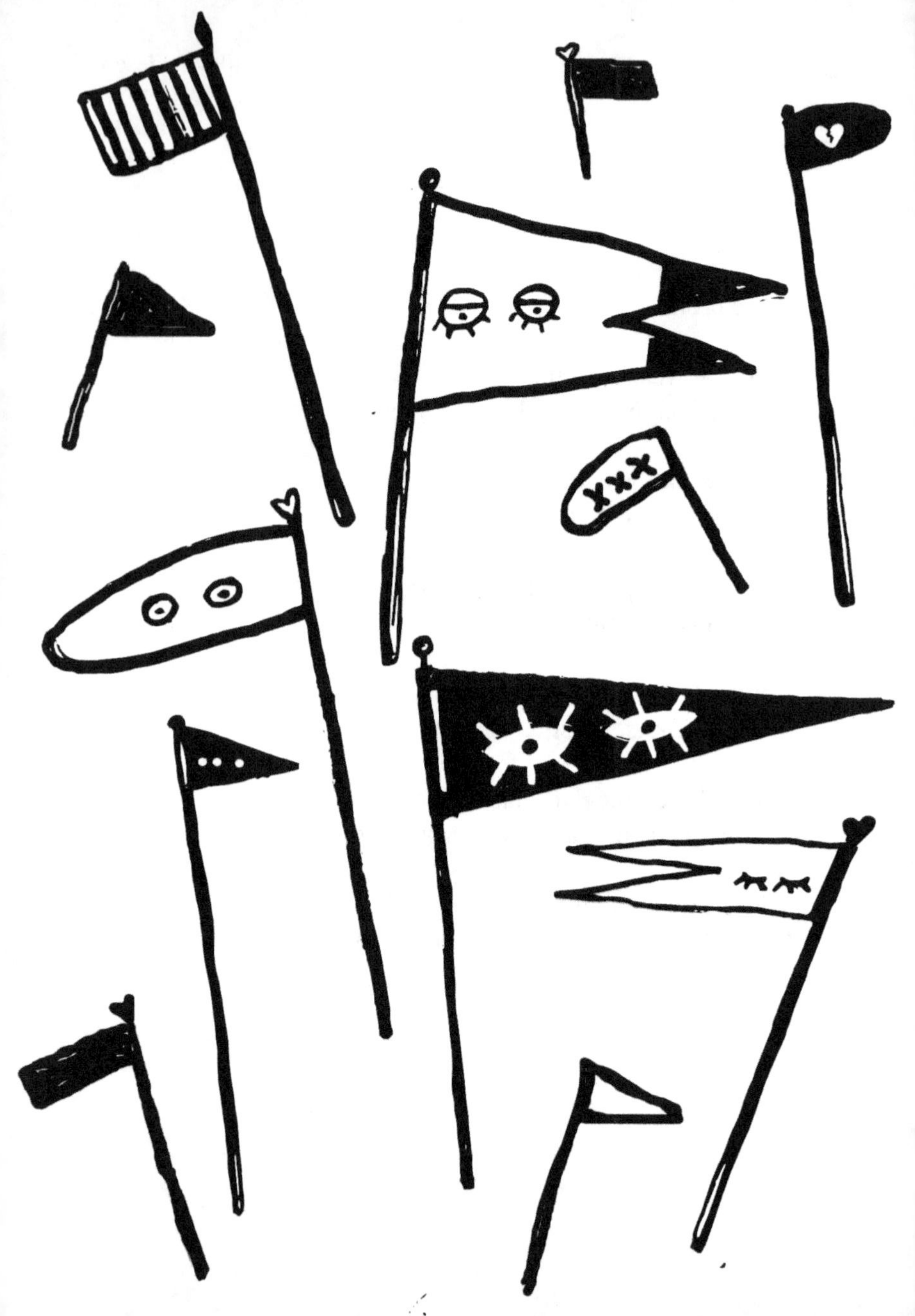

The Television as a Crystal Ball

All the summer bodies lay suctioned
to the sofa – barnacles upon a
sunken ship.

In the time of lies, we believed
in mermaids & remembered

when we saw them too –
scaled pixels flashing through the
static ocean.

It was only a Wellsian hoax

leaving us to make our own mermaids
of the fish among the swallowed
perfume bottles & cuckoo clocks –

the hauntings of the sea & the
intonations of white noise
on harlequin waves.

On The Virgin Suicides
[On *The Virgin Suicides*]

Obviously doctor, you've never been a thirteen-year-old girl.
– Cecilia Lisbon

Hail Mary,
I could never hold my peace.
I take a bath after I let him
take me.

My sister, full of grace,
puts the names of conquests
on her panties & I pray.
I think I'll do the same

& I pray harder, scrubbing
the thoughts from my wrists.
Mother on tub's ledge
sings "The Bridal Chorus"

& I confess everything
to the percolating faucet.
Ambrosial soaps coax blood
to my final baptism.

Psychic Reading in Moonstone

Numinous caravan propped in sediment – all the palm
prints rest against the pearl-glass sphere.

My hands burn & my hands squint
to see stags & crows running
towards my thumb.

It's not easy to read ghost hands – dead fortunes –

arterial rivers with realms
streaming off fingers into wells.

Blood only salts the breathing
future – lifelines grow new
legs to leave the corpse behind.

The Red Thread
[The Red Thread]

They call me queen of keeping my panties
full of minotaurs.

I've lined the thread of red
in public bathrooms across town.
You will follow me, pheromone-
man & ask me for my hand –

I was once transfixed by *Labyrinth*
shouting save the babe, selfish Sara –
& the babe is saved just in time.

Now, Goblin King, I love you
so follow me through
mirror-mouthed halls.

You'll tempt me with the taste of peach –
I'll kiss one of you with fists
of thread & send you
raveling back again.

Riding Hood

Little Red wasn't little
when she found apple-
blood in the cup of her
bloomers. She said *don't
call me little & don't call
me red. What big breasts
I have, risen like yeasty
loaves.* Big Bad Wolf
cat-calling all night,
but only she can stroke
the edge of her hood,
alone with the altruistic moon.
She'll don a little red sheath
when she says it's time,
sequins groping beams of light
as she skips past Granny's & howls
into a sap-stained forest of her own.

Up from the Salt Cellar

We all come from the inside
of a snake – the rat head
reanimates

the bowels & reveals
a fortune – my body,
naked

except for a crown
of amethyst & you
coming to make

a matryoshka doll
out of me – flick your
wrist against a shadow

& show me a star of a better
color, show me a
lunette infant

with a circus
for blood, show me
something that's never

seen a man & let it
fizz fast in celebratory
death. We all come

to die eventually & please
let my ghost wash smooth
as flat champagne.

The Most Beautiful Suicide

After the Photograph of Evelyn McHale

I wasn't there, but the sight of her is ice on my face –

She might have dressed at the mirror,
rouge & snood-haired for the event.
The city probably looked of stalagmites,
the lights dew-ooze from windows.

A limousine arrived as if to say that she,
having conquered the Nylon
Wars, deserves to die in style.

She had imagined herself chewed up
& brined with asphalt, indistinguishable
from plastic bags coated with rain-slime.

Instead, the body of the car became
a lake & Evelyn a dreamy swimmer
floating with clothes on.

The world still rippling
from her fizzled shout.

Kailey Tedesco

The Place Without Bodies
[The Place Without Bodies]

Everywhere is
            geometry & would you look
at the way those trees

arc forwards like ballerinas?   Would you look at me?
All of my life I was ballerina-
spread or girl-shaped

filled with only certain
colors. Of course I had flies
& I loved them –

they tugged at the vertex
of me, pulled me to non-
linearity – pulled me to

bottles of dirty pink soda I could
sleep in willingly.

            A man put me in a box

& he didn't know
I wasn't the box,
but I did & so did the flies.

In Old Hollywood

I spin fast & fall
into freshly vacuumed
ceilings.   Here,

they call me *Mirror, Mirror*
& treat my body
like a frame

they can't hang
straight & I yank out
hair like exorcisms.

Their mansions & mine
hold hands in quiet
seance & wait

for the wake of ectoplasm
in the form of stars
in the form

of the girl who's gone
missing from her Kansas
city trailer & whose Mama

calls *Justine, if you can hear
me, come home so my peripheral
might stop smelling your body*

in the corpses of leaves.
All the while my name is
changed like the wet

infant left on the pavement
at daybreak & now they
call us both   *baby.*

I Hear Evil Enter Through the Nothing of Me
[I Hear Evil Enter Through the Nothing of Me]

I.

I am siamese (because I choose to be)
& always pregnant – it's true
I ate the rabbit's innards & I ate
the caul.

I wish I were siamese with the statue
of Mary – I crawl inside her
voided eye & see

myself curled in cement
at the corner of the garden & I am

so full.

II.

I am always two
or three things – I was born inside
another woman
& she said I felt like a ouija board

or a bi-level house with
a murder inside.

There were not one
but two Eves & the serpent. I think
I'm still inside the serpent – I was born
into a sack of divination &

there are so many windows
to shut.

III.

When I'm here, I talk
in reverse.

Sleep in the guff makes me wake up
beautiful & I bring you
to bed –

You are inside me with everything
tugging you further – the jungle

of my innards wants
to maul you

& bring you to the heaven
of me.

I am afraid
in heaven I will not cry.

Kailey Tedesco

Room at The Madonna Inn

The dirt worries someone may knock soon
Can you hear the gong? Someone is at the door   dancing
(mirror-bones scattered on the floor)

Gilt shards – a bee's wings blitz through hotel meadows
Narwhals in the basement sleep   & eat in glass skeletons

Carpet forests of fake stars shaking the trees like real winds
There is nothing on my plate   nothing to eat

The cinema plays *La Double Vie de Veronique*
She & She   the teeth between scarlet curtains

The cinemas all stop
shush
can't you hear the real bees?

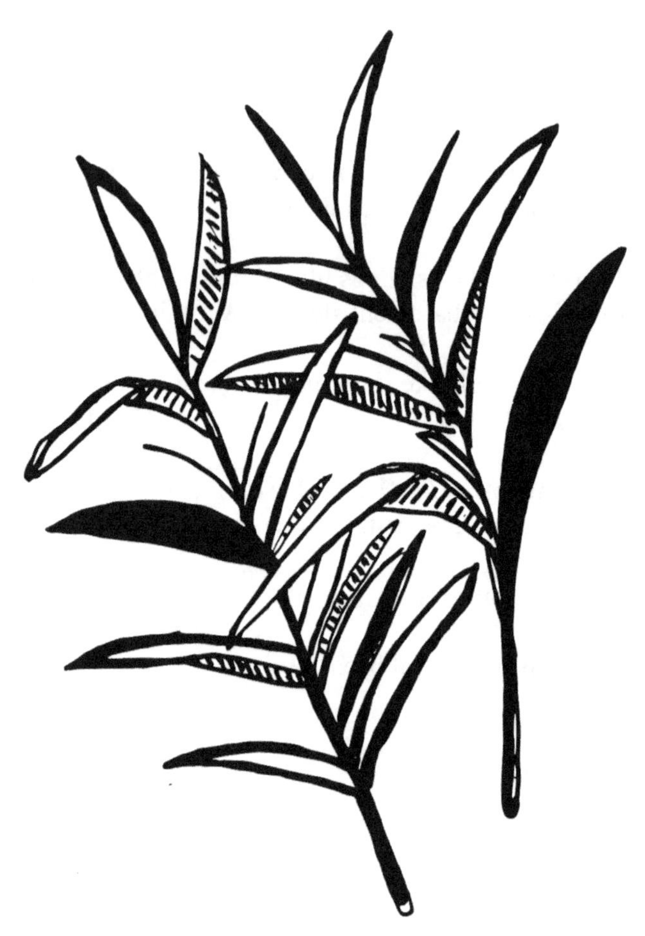

Kailey Tedesco

The Way His Aura Feels
[The Way His Aura Feels]

Sometimes honey on tongues,
un-sucked.

It's there. Dangling the way
gnats lay – tinsel on branches
of air –

poking me in shiver-spots,
ducking from my sock-in-
the-eye attempts.

Sometimes it's water skin you don't
notice until your hand is
stuck.

It's something inside of me,
not pulsing around,

still in my mouth as I prod it.

A Brothel in Rose Quartz

        Feels like sitting in another's aura —
pink ectoplasm bubble-stuffed
with ghost girls.

They lounge on velvet furniture
like discarded kimonos, druzy with the sweat
of bug-zapper Septembers.

All's tassels & masquerade among
the magazine's spinning perfumes.
With not a man in sight,

it is beautiful to be the Madame
of the phantomed & watch heaven
spill from the parlor fans.

How Often We Confuse Ovens for Rabbit Holes

In grocery stores, I hate the smell of raw
roses by the dozen. Suddenly I'm seven

& you're pulling me out of school, or I'm
fourteen & the mortician hands me a tissue

that I hold, unblown, like my friend, *light-
as-a-feather-stiff-as-a-board*. What I'm getting

at is I'm sick of sitting in pews doused with
grocery store petals – they affront & I'm sucked

into a whirlwind of pollen. It's disturbing how
stamen can make such associations, but I can't

get the local magician out of my head. He pulled
a carnation from his lopsided top hat, elastic strung

haphazardly around his unshaven mug. As he extends
the flower, his face too close to mine, I wonder if he

wears the top hat all of the time – even while eating
beer-dipped sardines poolside? Did I ever tell you

I used to play in the carcasses of whales? They were
washed up all over the tree-line & I, in my

communion socks, counted the paces from mouth
to tail until the whales became too stuffed with

fungus or the magician pulled up in his rose
gold Hyundai to ask me if I need a ride. A good

witch won't offer you chewing gum & I'm not
crawling in, but I am fattening up. And we can

spend our whole lives shouting Bloody Mary
into mirrors, hoping she'll pop by & bring

us through the other side, but chrome is as murky
as any above-ground pool. All my life, I've been

chasing the vermin home, only to wake up
exactly where I started.

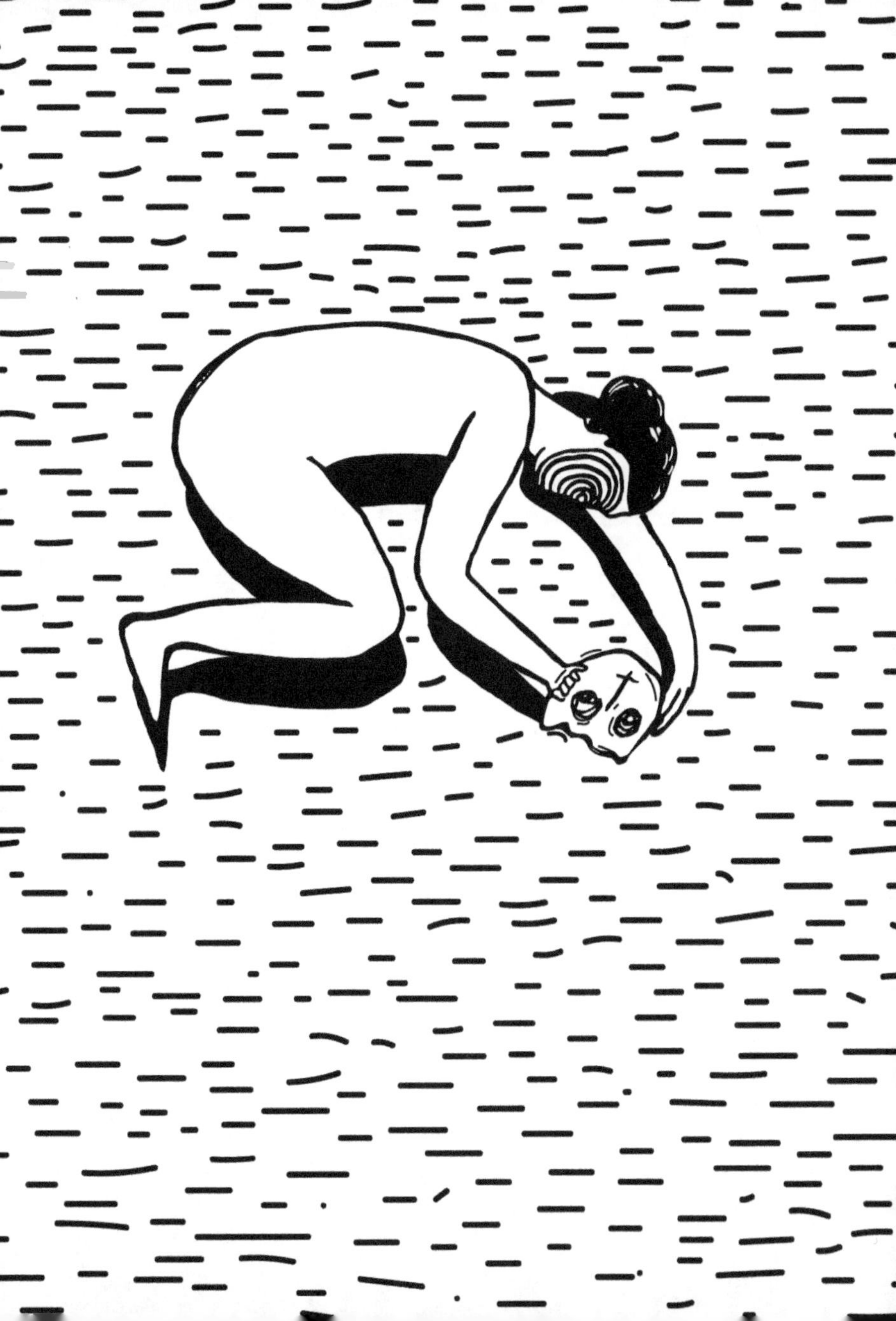

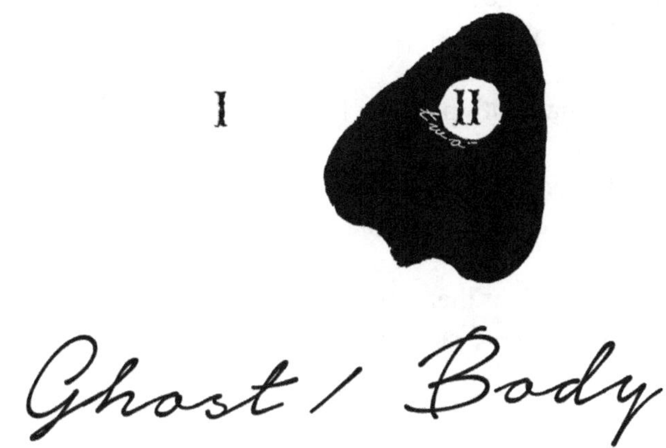

Ghost / Body

[Ghost / Body]

The Place After Crossing Over

I have two candles

     mashed mandrakes in my womb

from birth – one is not born
unless one becomes

     a woman with phoenix hair

feathers & fire & my two candles
only two candles left to call God with

& no matches to light them, but
hair alight with red – dead feathers

& ash

left over, left under my feet the way light
caresses my shadow one final time, the way

I disturb the light once more before returning

     the way it juniors itself to me to ask for
     one last dance in front of windows – curtains open

once more before I return the light of me
like coin-debts to the jangling [blank]

it came from.

She Used to Be on a Milk Carton

I hear Her in my conch shell –

The girl who has the moon stuck between
Her teeth like the wedge of an orange.

This girl is all moon, I think, because I've seen Her
spin the ocean like a skirt about Her waist.

When asked where she belongs she says *anywhere
but the sky* & that she misses Her pearls –

God, where are they?
She was pleased when I handed Her a costume

strand – stars clasped behind Her neck.
I roll them between my finger & thumb, wait

for beads to come skittering through
the streets with a single tug.

Girl Shaped Like an Axe Murderer

        glitches above intertidal shards –
glass unswept & gorgeous
at a distance – God liked my

sins, so he kept them secret
in a box out by his shed. My grandmother said
it is unholy to spread

tarot over chapel stoops,
but sometimes dark on grass feels
too much like an eyelid. I live

with bloody children – I live with a master
list of all the shrines
to see before I die. Now I live,

but I will die & I'm sorry
for it – put my ghost inside peacock
ore & worship. Worship the way

mirrors feel when covered
in polaroid & ribbon. Let me die
apologetically as a feathered thing

with bones in my eyes & a crown
of caul. Let me find lostness in
this forest & count the killers,

Kailey Tedesco

their mouths stuffed
with the gelatin of sky
between tree & tree & tree.

The Purgatory Choice

In the mud-angel beneath my body's
last defenses lies Her contract. I can feel it
roll over me like galaxies

& I am blinded from

his hair-gnarled hands & the give
of my elbows, the gel of my ghost pressed
cheek-to-cheek with my own
seizing body.

Her wants to eat me & Her wants kill me
herself like a mother. She'll put me
deep in a place I can't remember
while re-runs play on TV.

I say yes & I say it quickly.

Promise Ring
[Promise Ring]

The grass-scratch
of the End cuts
my belly dry & empty –
I climb over

hedgerows & into living
spaces with hexagonal
papers – the moose-bust
on my finger rots

the way to 24-Hour Video.
Through a pinned-
jaw, it tells me to hide
behind the romances. A gunman
hides always inside glass
eyes – he wants

my face to pry open
in stop-motion – he wants
my game, but I lick
the antlers clean. I leave
carcass-escrow for
my girl with dark hair

so in the End
she'll have bones
that are not her own

to suck dry.

On Picnic at Hanging Rock
[On *Picnic at Hanging Rock*]

Everything begins and ends at the exactly right time and place.
– Joan Lindsey

Sometimes I am in Australia
& the Everywhen kept lodged in rock.

I asked my ex-boyfriend what it was like –

he said sit still & contemplate the black river pearls.
They looked like flecks of empty space.

If I could just phone Her from whatever
plane she's on & ask what time is it there?

Is it possible to just want to believe that she
threw corsets so she might dance

as she pleased elsewhere? The reality might be
that she's simply cutting the same

Saint Valentine cake again & again.

Kailey Tedesco

The Debut of a Lady in White

It was the night of the stripped mattress
& your smile shaped like a

guillotine reflecting waves of
teeth – first you had ceramic worms

to put inside me like decorations,
spaced evenly so they'd glimmer like

lava lamps with a flick of a switch. Then red
garlands to be cleaned with globs of

last year's suntan when I stayed under
water even though my mother called

& called.   Last, the licks
of damask-set furnaces. You re-dressed me

in an urn & made me hate the word
"urinal," but every burial, be it metaphoric

or not, begets something
again & again like an old set of

matryoshka dolls haunting the path
of your rearview mirror.

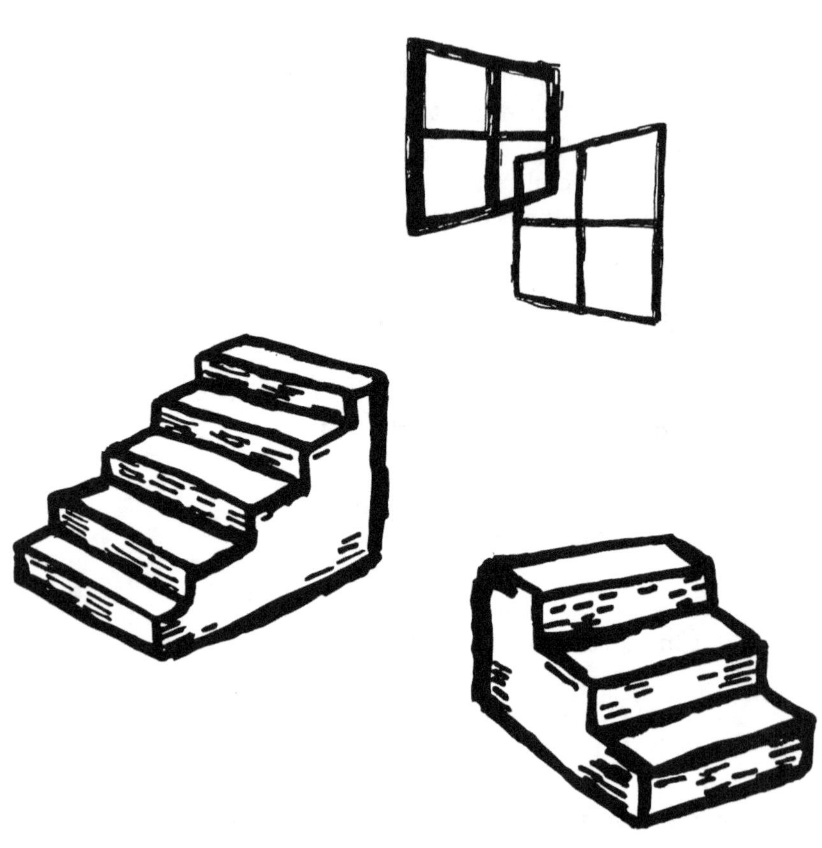

These Ghosts of Mine, Siamese

How long have you been waking
in my sternum? A grandmother
of mine had a set of uteri –

one for the living & one for
the heads of specters goitered

softly to my bra-bones. Every day
you sip my death with an orange

juice breakfast & I feel it.   A witch
of mine said to dowse you out, so I

found the forked twig that best resembled
my future tearing from my past –

a midway geek with compass hands.   No one
of mine will believe in *Dark Shadows*

mythologies, but trust in the whipped yolks
of my eyes once sea-blackened with moon.

If Hell Had a Body

[If Hell Had a Body]

You taste of bavarian & I cannot
get your gardenia-limbs

to fold the same –
I've made magic circles

out of your jalousie-
eyes & if I could, I would

crawl inside you like church.
I would take in pastille

air with groin-pleasure
until I found myself submerged

in the lake where you held
my head underwater –

that day I could hear the lilies
& they said get out soon

it is so hot.

Then Back to the Abyss She Fell

Do you remember the exhibit in the
Mütter Museum?

The mummified child whose eye-
lashes stayed full, her skin grey & supple.

I can understand the look on her face now –
like pretending to be asleep.

My forested body's own pruned lids
lay similarly porcelain with doll lashes,
un-flickering.

Inside, the stuff of me has scurried
off to play pretend with dried twigs.
Imagine magic wands in my hands –

the force of moments where
the sprigs can manipulate
the wash of time.

Dollhouse on Unmarked Grave

Objects of natural disaster can be measured
only in functionality – the dead

bear: a pile of dried wine & twig-
maggots rocking themselves

in small circles – I make

contact for the purpose
of classification & the swirling

ghosts   of things   gone

useless, limp, not
awake, but more

awake   more wide & in place

than the chimney that careens itself
upwards & into skies that turn

green & sire   washing

the emptied bear

creating   gone-ness

& the odor of

        birth.

The Difference Between Life and Death is Antlers

After death, we can see antlers
are as natural as hair groping

static. Our memories dangle from
the rack like wrinkled balloons –

horrible things strung with an electricity
she cannot see.

She takes last breaths stuffed with
missing posters & hangs

the exhale like wool coats so
we must tiptoe to look murder in the eye.

From far away, the antlers are plaits
enchanted with tea roses & glass barrettes.

Up close, they're the day Earth hocked
us out & everything

that comes after.

Cemetery in Lemon Chrysoprase

A tetragonal labyrinth scries *walk, walk* –
It says it rains during funerals because

the earth turns & the jagged edges
pierce the ears of sky. It chants – *I don't*

know, I don't. The lyme in this place
matches the carnation I toss in,

matches the color of your skin at the
end, matches the sun that absorbs, not leaks

light – a common misconception. Here is your
catechism: do you have nickels on your eyes,

or the rosary's plasticine in your hair? Yes?
Yes – We drink of this froth, sour & plenty.

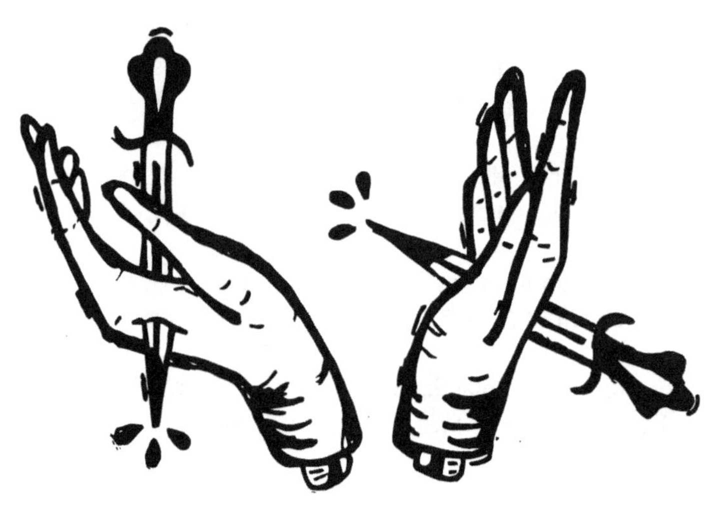

God in Real Life

accepts my collect calls & *man*, do I gab!

Phone-coils wrapped around prayer hands, I ask
Do horrible things have thoughts before they happen?

*Do they yell "Stop, you people!" & try to arrange
everyone back in their assigned seats?*

God showed up in the form of a chick I wanted to hold.
The chick grew a beak with teeth & pecked my hand to shreds

that reminded me of pet bedding in a cage. I felt guilty
in that moment for all the hamsters I ever forgot to feed.

Everyone yelled *kill it!* & I almost wanted to –
one snap & it'd be lint dirtying the floor.

But I let us both cry out, because wasn't it me
who wanted to hold the creature to begin with?

I Don't Want to Talk About the Man

His face, crudely
taped to my front door –

I have seen him
in the deli aisles where I keep
my gaze down & recite
we-don't-trick-or-treat
on-Fern Street –

I often sink into my
chair these days –
hidden from mole-
nosed stars that wrinkle
& pucker against
my window as horn-tailed
rains splash down.

Why, I wonder, is it
so hard to be untouched?

Francesca's Tour of the Female Inferno

[Francesca's Tour of the Female Inferno]

It is so easy to forget
I look nothing like my mother –

how many worlds are stuffed
into my mouth this morning & with what

did you engorge me? A bed full
of something sweetened with familiarity,

probably. Dirt levitates within me
like sleeping girls. My consistency is that

of courtesan bedroom canopies & cabbage
roses dolloping walls at grand hotels.

I am smoke staring earnestly at fog
in disbelief that we've been separated

all our lives & are just now meeting
at summer camp – each of us deciduous

as celluloid turning through
hot pupils of wind.

Eureka's Coven
[Eureka's Coven]

September esbat & I met Her for tea –

She unwraps weather & hands me a piece.
We pop thunderstorms like chewing gum, spit
the sopping membranes into cups.

Lipstick ground, we drink down & let
luna moths alight in our hips.

I swallow, hail & all, & feel blood-
orange lilies take root under lungs' shade.

I speak now in breaths of pink lemonade
& lightning freckles my eyes.

Studies Find Pearls Are Teeth After All

I've never been in woods
without the sight of interstates,

but I want to be so lost I lose
the diagram of my own form

among forest circles echoing
from tree-flesh

in small eternities. I am always half-
hoping to find an eye-plucked body

so I can be the hero who arrived
too late — a bad witch, or the not-

sound of every branch encasing
me in an oyster shell

where I will stay Hammurabi-handless
with agate nubs, not quite

a dead fish. Who can remember
those other lives

where I swam with my egg-tooth
out proud? I wake up

She Used to Be on a Milk Carton

with dead teeth
in my fist – I'll shuck them

like roses & let them grow
skins of their own.

The Witch Practices Spells for Loosening the Noose

Last night Eureka's teeth powdered
like pressed glass & we saw Her grinding

on the roof with bees by the dozens –
hovering to the beats of generators,

honeying the gardens with ghosts gone
ambered & lazed.

We saw Her & she didn't see us looking
like beasts even when we yellowed our eyes –

She's had eternities to be the hunter & hunted,
but in every story she rises with the surge of gem-blood

flooding hard stone, dragging the down
of Her own pelt behind Her.

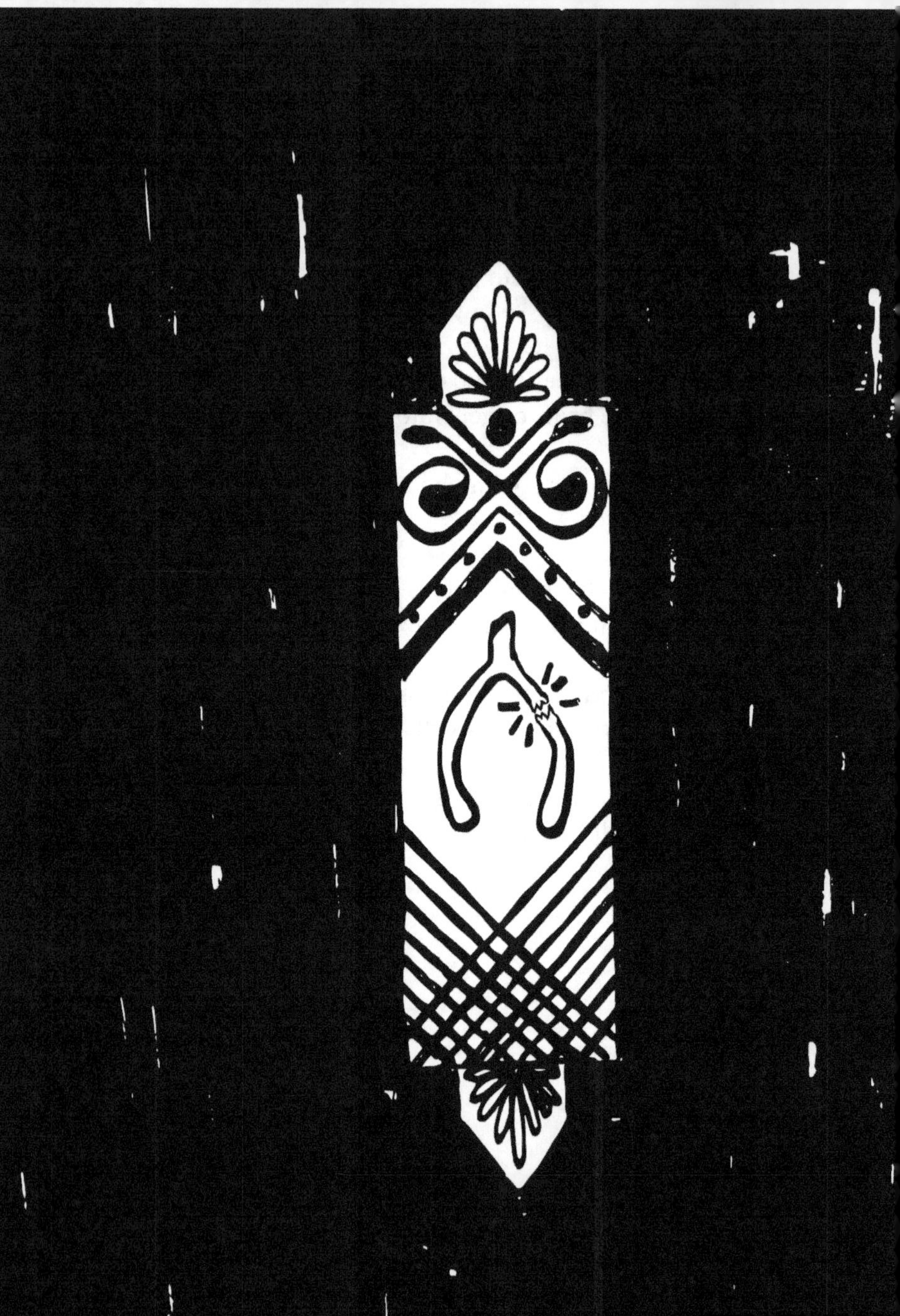

The Textbooks Will Tell You the Moon is a Face

[The Textbooks Will Tell You the Moon is a Face]

I know this isn't true. It's more of a knee-cap
flexing itself back-and-forth so that it might
kick the stars about.

Stones are only stones.

No. I can creak them open like rust lockets
& expose the chunks of sea inside,
all crag & ice boned.

You see black when your eyes are closed.

Black is not always nothing, though. Sometimes,
you'll see a full sky – a murder or a cloud.

Oh, Adored Cadaver
[Oh, Adored Cadaver]

Wind your astrolabe – let it tick
like the stick of thighs emerging from
a hot bath.

Be happy in your body
sans circulation, purpled like cock-
flesh & in bed with one calve

outstretched. Maybe an exaggeration.
But behind glass nonetheless, or a

shrine to math. Add: the times he
watched as you nearly awoken

& every Saint to light his prayer
at your portrait. There are stars

that aren't eyes. I promise.
More importantly, the ocean's
an ovary & it's on your side.

Kailey Tedesco

Don't cry – let whale breath
suck at the toes of your own
lovely skeleton & then

laugh & then close. Remind
him how horrible Rapunzel

hair reeks when it grows.

The Moth Cycle

My grandmother's lake & a girl
on her belly.

Her damp hands peel moss
from earth, disturb
the mushrooms.

Small moth's stir –

she adjusts her swimsuit & pounces,
pansies in her fist &

a crumple of white wings
petal-frail.

Day's end lines her game along the tide. One lap
carries the bodies, easily as wind.

Somewhere across the lake – my body
blood-stiff & grey with rain.

Glassy wings stream
from the vague instar of my skull.

Ophelia as Lazarus

A water garden snakes
up through the throat & chokes
on St. Anthony's prayer – that dampness

blanketing lungs, seeds sprout
faster than usual. It is always
faster than it usually is. It was

believed I would grow
to doppel
a Hepburn, though it wasn't

specified which – it was believed
I would survive the drowning. After all
the caul bathed me before

you did – but Stepmother,
but Beldam, but Man with axe
& heart-box. I know it had

to be a trinity to web
my voice with florets,
dilating my bones

with oak flutes that betray
your clandestine & reveal
wisps of red hair

curling up from the bottom
of the well.

Kailey Tedesco

It is December in My Hands

[It is December in My Hands]

They are the newsprint of

the sky at morning commute. Ducks
have flown, the water's

flow has halted as figure
skaters arabesque carving

the lines inside my palms
& still I grin at red cracks –

cardinals stamping the white.

Kailey Tedesco

Everything Abandoned Must Go On

You cannot hear or see
dancers on plush carpets.

The katydids will cover the walls
with grand pliés –

I like remembering wolverines
sprawled in bathtubs,

large branches spying
like the Queen of Wands.

It won't matter if you leave
the faucets on. One day they may

resume their can-can pragmatism
& douse the curtains in hibiscus liquid.

These rooms trace a cross
on their foreheads.

A mattress curls & sucks
its thumb.

Let the chandeliers
salt the floorboards —

These are our last rites.

Mood Ring

Stuff the Michelangelo sky
into a blender, letting cotton-
pink wisp like child-curls.

Make a cup of tea. Take the
tentacle swirl of cream's first
kiss with black-steep & freeze.

With a pipette, extract the summer
sky over green lights & billboards,
grind night's freckles into fine

powder, slice a piece of the sun
(careful not to break the crust)
& fold over egg yokes.

Pluck a single bead of water
from a midnight bath & inject
the gem with color.

Can There Be God Without Ghosts?

[Can There Be God Without Ghosts?]

I cry about this & the nihilism in orbs that are all flash.

Horror always makes me believe harder –
Danny got the Shining somewhere & I think

it was given to him the same way I prayed for a snow
day & it happened, or how I said take

my hair in exchange & thanked God
the drain was clogged.

My mother says I'm a caulbearer & God is in that. Maybe
not in my being a caul-bearer, but in my mother who says I am.

God's not the Shining, or the slayer, or the clairvoyant who
gives five dollar readings, but God is the way they assert

themselves as such – shawl-clad & powerful people who
clutch at rosaries & won't tell you

it was just the wind.

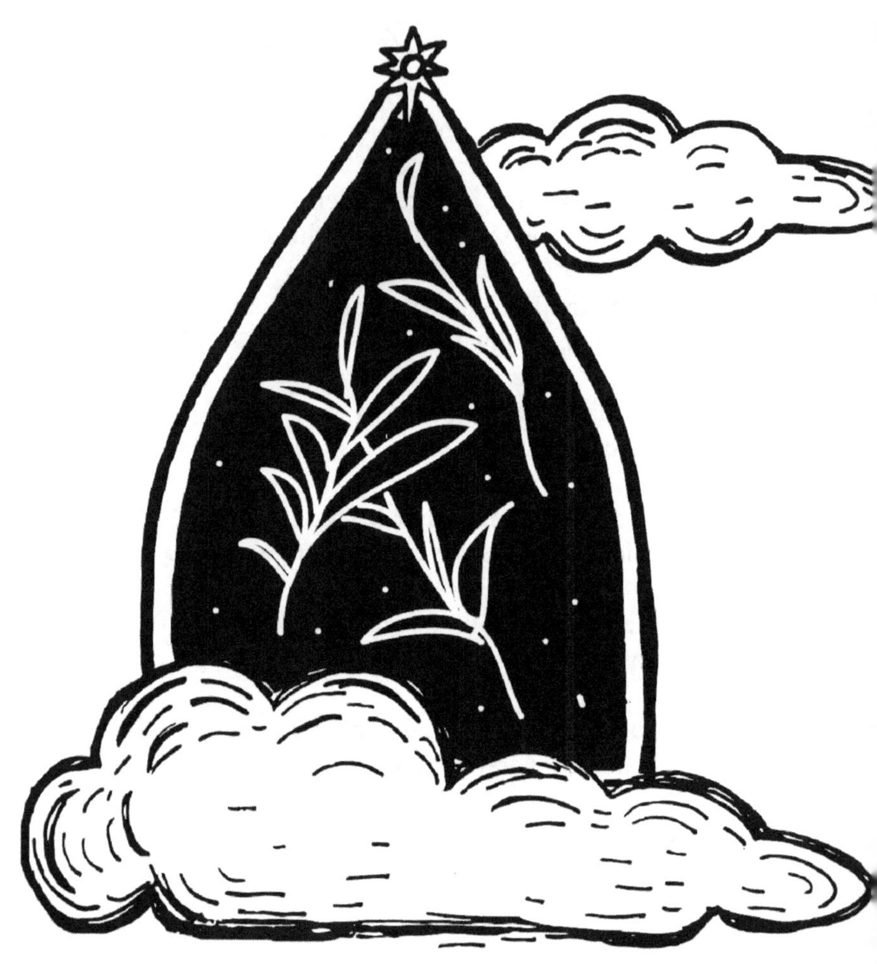

Kailey Tedesco

Resurrection of the Fawn

I was meadow-minded to think gravel was only a creek-leap.
She didn't see me running, just coming into my own legs –
nothing but knuckles in Her arms.

Roadside with spine-weaved flesh & eyes wet, Her rings catch
my velvet as she connects the spots on my back, kissing the blood-
scent from my nose.

With moss-breath still in Her lap, she watches my bone-memory
resume and crank me, body-upright,
bend by bend.

When All the Trees Go Up in Flames,
Only Water Puts Them Back to Sleep

I held the forest
like a hairbrush in
one hand & my
grandmother's pond
like a hand-mirror.

With my vanity set
lifted gently from
the alabaster of earth
I spend seven years
combing through

the tangles of my fire-
streaked hair as fallen
strands puddle in the under-
growth.

A reflection ripples
over drowsed eyelids –
the foxes wake to hunt.

Witch Fingers

They stretched first upwards – cold branches
combing the brow of sky – then at me
all crack-boned & ready to snap.

You know witch fingers by bones that recoil
and ejaculate magic like horseflies. She said
she'll cast embryos –

put them in a hole like a dead swimming pool
stuffed with citrine gel & the bloat
of the pink bear I once rescued from the lake.

I lift that bear now, in reverse-baptism –
scream when tadpoles stream from plush
ears and writhe across my knuckles.

The hole in the world was a grave
& the fingers, still sputtering dust clouds,
will be the last to fold in bloom antipode.

Acknowledgements

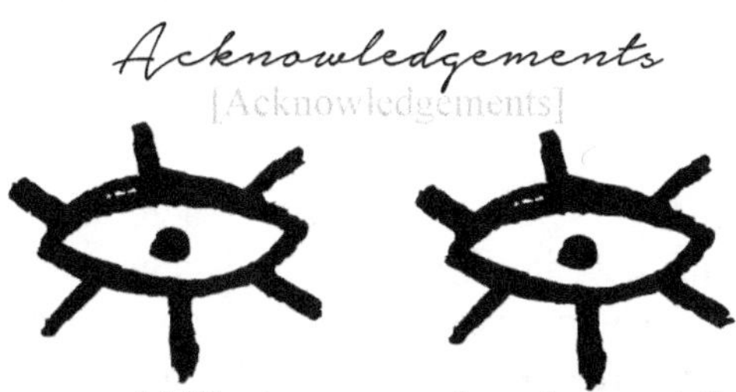

The author would like to express her sincerest thanks to the following literary journals where the poems in this book first appeared, sometimes under a different title or in an earlier form:

FLAPPERHOUSE, *Lehigh Valley Vanguard, Boston Poetry Magazine,* Wicked Banshee Press, Jersey Devil Press, *Hermeneutic Chaos,* Rising Phoenix Press, *Eternal Haunted Summer, Menacing Hedge, Yellow Chair Review, Up the Staircase Quarterly, Bop Dead City, Rust + Moth, After the Pause, Broadkill Review, Luna Luna Magazine, Prick of the Spindle, Waxing & Waning, Vanilla Sex Magazine, Minola Review, Five to One Magazine, Rogue Agent, Rose Red Review, Reality Beach, Milkfist Magazine, Prelude, Crack the Spine, Modern Poetry Quarterly Review, Quail Bell Magazine, Hypertrophic Literary,* The Opiate, *Sugar House Review, American Chordata, Bad Pony, Yes, Poetry, Meat for Tea,* and *Poetry Quarterly.*

Thank you to Poems-for-All for turning "How Often We Confuse Ovens for Rabbit Holes" (originally published by FLAPPERHOUSE) into a poetry booklet.

Thank you to Dancing Girl Press for publishing my chapbook, *These Ghosts of Mine, Siamese* (2016), where some of the poems in this collection have appeared.

Thank you, too, to Samara, Robert, Zach, and Emily for being the family Roald Dahl protagonists would likely fantasize about. Thank you to Joey for calling out sick to make every one of my readings. Thank you to my Grandma Mary for introducing me to my own imagination. Thank you to my MFA cohort at Arcadia University – without Michelle, Mike, Chad, Dorian, and Jim, this collection would surely not exist. Special thanks to Professor Genevieve Betts who spent hours combing through this manuscript and treating it like her own. Thank you to everything wonderfully strange that has ever happened to me and to everyone who is kinda wonderfully strange themselves.

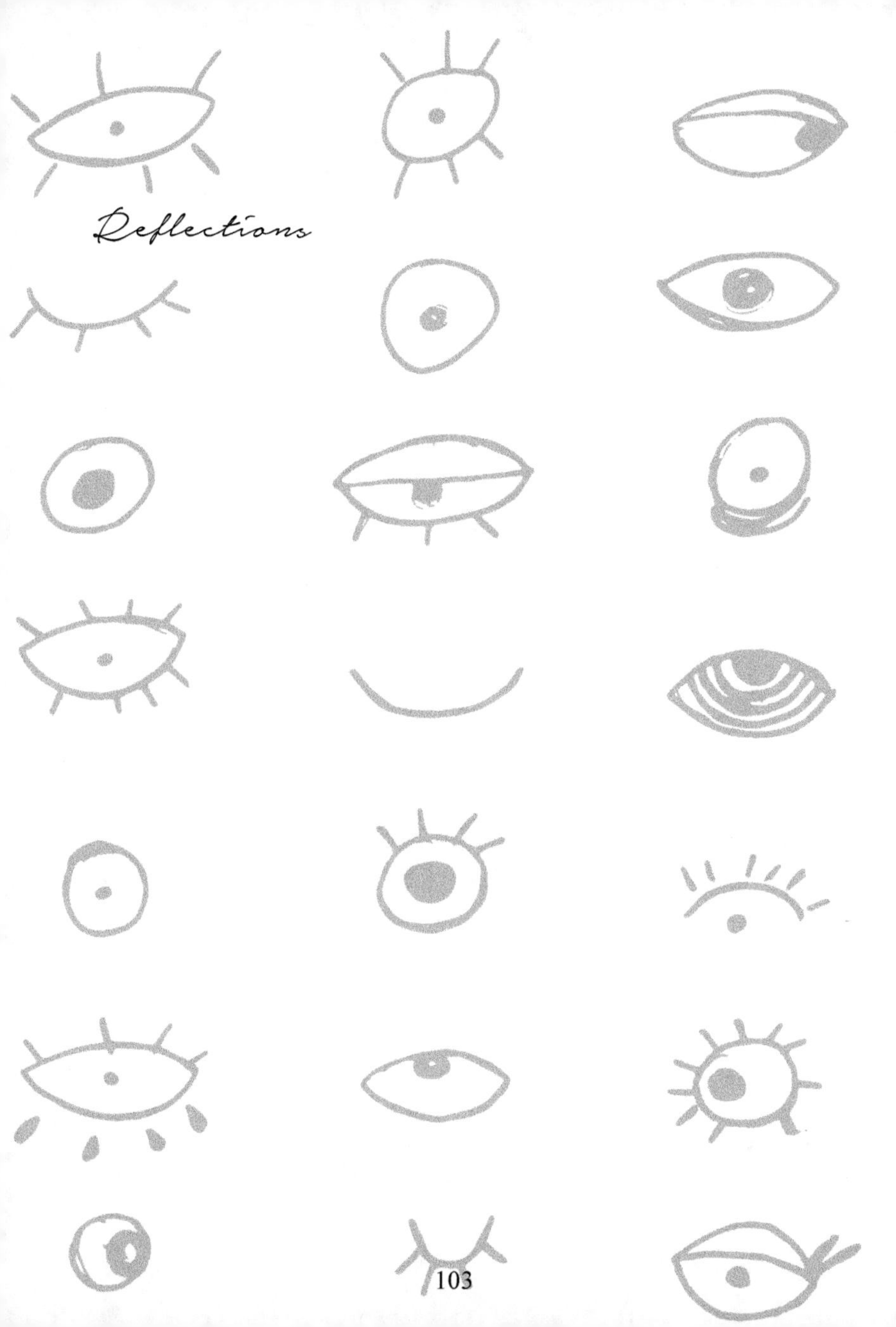
Reflections

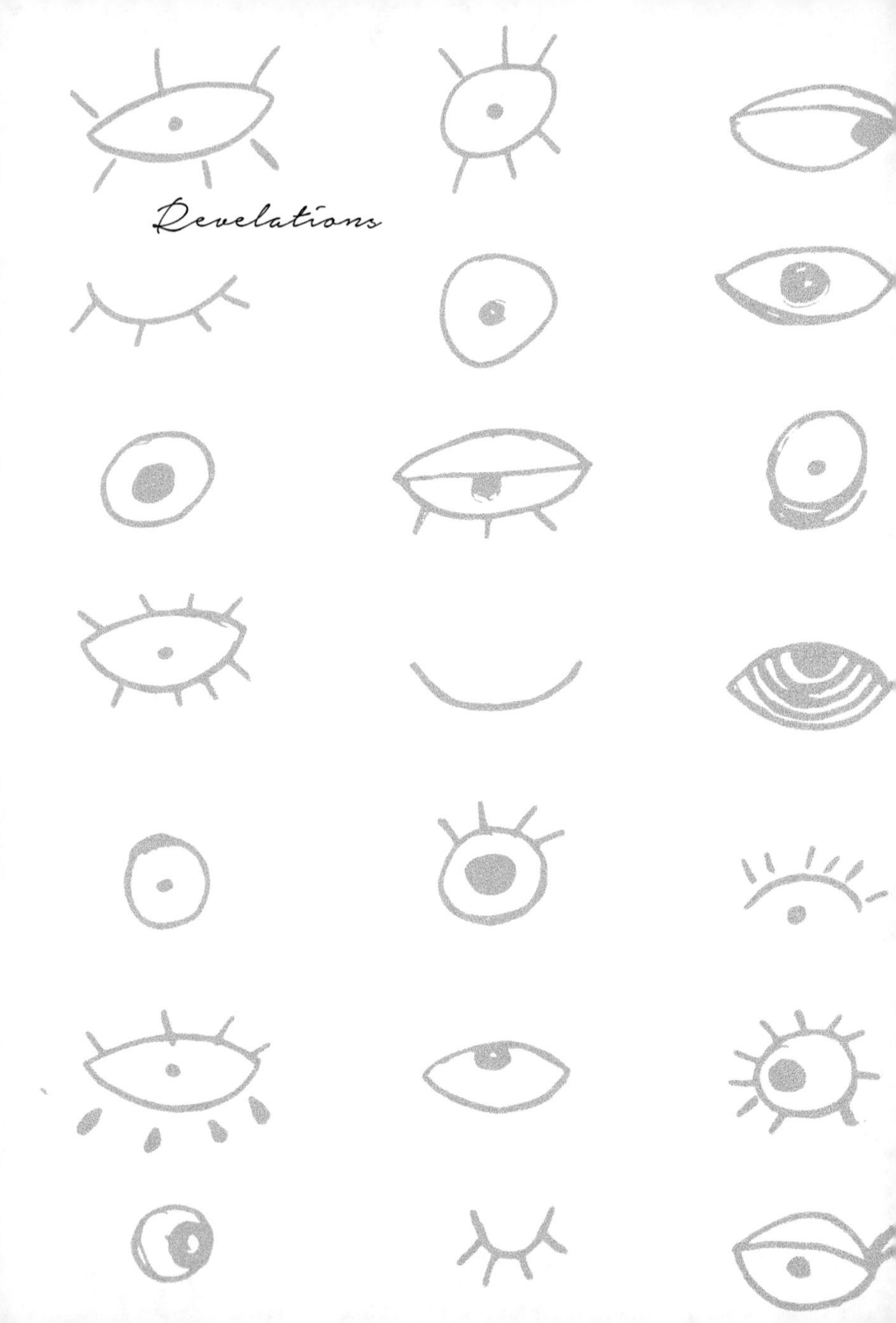

Revelations